L'ABRI
At The Beginning

The Schaeffers & L'Abri
1955 - 1956

Sandra Sweeny Silver

ISBN: 9798746771070

Front Cover Image: L'Abri - Chalet Les Melezes

Also By Sandra Sweeny Silver

NONFICTION

The Rise And Fall Of The House Of Herod
Footprints In Parchment: Rome Versus Christianity 30-313 AD
Pocket Full Of Posies
A Cosmos In My Kitchen: The Diary Of A Beekeeper
Abortion: A Biblical Consideration
The—Trust Me On This—Really Good Food Cookbook
Blog on Rome and the Early Christians:
www.earlychurchhistory.org

FICTION

Snowtime
Just A Little Short

Dedicated to the memory of Francis & Edith Schaeffer

And to their children - Priscilla, Susan, Debby, Frank

CONTENTS

L'ABRI AT THE BEGINNING

CHAPTER 1
HEIDI COUNTRY

On a Sunday evening in May of 1984 I was teaching the Book of Revelation in the Bible to about 50 people in the Carriage House behind our home in Ridgefield, Connecticut. My husband Steve and I had a Bible Study there every Sunday night for many years. People from churches in our surrounding communities came at 6:30 PM. We often had pot luck dinners. I feel food is a necessity for good Bible Studies as we feed on the Food of Life. Many in the group brought friends who did not know the Lord and I picked up a few people in the supermarket and on the street. We always finished at 9:00 PM. As we mingled that Sunday, someone came up to me and said, "You've probably heard, Sandy, that Francis Schaeffer just died." I had not heard. Immediately I went upstairs to be alone and cried. Some time later I rejoined the group, got up to teach and said: "None of you would be in this room without Francis Schaefer who just died."

Some of the people in the room knew the name Francis Schaeffer and some did not. I told them: "Francis Schaeffer and his wife Edith were the ones who brought me to the Lord. Without the Lord in my life, we would not be here together reading and studying God's Word."
At age 18 how did I get from my home in Mt. Lebanon, Pennsylvania in August of 1955 all the way to Huemoz, Switzerland, to L'Abri which the Schaeffers had just started in June of 1955?
Our Rec room in Mt. Lebanon was in the basement of our Victorian home. "Rec rooms," recreation rooms, were very popular in the 1950's and when I became a teenager, my parents made part of our basement into a place where I could be alone with my friends. Some of my friends had very elaborate Rec rooms with mini-bars stocked with cokes and carpets and comfortable couches and good lights. Ours was not like that, but it was a place where our clique could hang out. Each class in the 50's had cliques. The dictionary definition of "clique" is "a small group of people, with shared interests or other features in common, who spend time together and do not readily allow others to join them." By my Senior Year in high school, there were ten of us girls and ten boys who were "popular." The girls were all "cute" and were majorettes or cheerleaders. The boys were mainly football players. One of

the football players once came to us in my Junior Year and asked us to allow his girlfriend to be a member of our group. There were pros and cons among us. I think that was the first time I thought, "Gee, there's something strange and wrong here." She was allowed in as long as she dated him. Lest one think that hierarchy was a 50's phenomenon, it is still there in all groups of people—elementary schools, middle schools, high schools, colleges, country clubs, offices, neighborhoods….

I had always been an "inside" person. At school, I was Sandy the peppy, funny, cute little blond cheerleader who spoke what they called "50 cent words," meaning I used words others did not know. My Mother told me never to allow people to change the way I was and never "to speak down to others." It was she who had taught me when I was a rebellious child and told people to "shut up," to say instead to them "the exuberance of your verbosity is opprobrious" and that would shut them up. I did say that to several people who annoyed me as a young child, but by Senior High, I was not tempted to tell people to shut up.

I would come home from school, go up to my cozy bedroom on the third floor of our home, open my books and learn things. By age 10-11, I had looked around me and thought, "What's this all about? What's the meaning in all of this? What's the truth, the real TRUTH in all of this living and in those stars so far away and in just the plain everyday life of eating, drinking, talking we all do?"

I first turned to Poetry. It was my first literary LOVE. I memorized Longfellow, Poe, Browning. I found comfort in rhyming verses and their poetic truths. In Mrs. Reed's 5th grade class in Alliance, Ohio, she said if anyone "wanted to go down in history," he should decipher the Mayan hieroglyphs. When I got home that day, I told my Mother I wanted a book on the Mayans. For Christmas she gave me Sylvanus Griswold Morley's book *The Ancient Maya*. I dog-eared that book and became interested in archaeology. The more I studied, the more I realized that all the ancients— the Mayans, Aztecs, Incas, the Greeks, Romans, Babylonians, Phoenicians, Egyptians—were just like we are today but they did not have cars or electricity.

I don't remember how I first came upon Albert Camus' *The Myth Of Sisyphus And Other Essays*. When I read *The Myth Of Sisyphus* at about 15, I had found truth. Even though man, Sisyphus, is condemned by the gods to do a meaning-less task all his life, we "must imagine Sisyphus happy" as he stands upon the mountain and watches the boulder roll down again. And he KNOWS he must go down and roll it up again. Yes, those of us who KNOW life is illogical are above all the rabble who do not KNOW that truth. That is why Sisyphus is happy as he watches the boulder roll down the hill and knows he has to go down and roll it up again—for eternity. That is why only the "knowledge-filled" are happy, satisfied because they know all life is absurd.

I read some of Sartre, but did not like him. Camus was my man. He condemned suicide as an alternative to living without purpose. Did he kill himself on purpose when he ran into that tree in 1960? Did "life without meaning" get to him in the end? Maybe.

Nevertheless, when Dad and I were in our Rec room that evening of my Senior Year in high school, we were discussing where I wanted to go to college. It was tacitly implied I would go to Denison where all my mother's brothers had gone. I had once mentioned I might like to go to the University of Chicago, but my parents were adamantly against that. By that time I had determined I did not want to go to a college in the United States. I wanted to go far away to Europe or somewhere else to study. I needed time alone from every one and every thing I knew so that I could continue my search for truth with a capital "T."

"Sandra, where are you thinking about going to college?" Dad asked.

"I don't want to go to college in America. I want either to go to college in Europe or go into a nunnery for a while." I said.

"You're not going to be a goddamned nun!" We were not even Catholic, but I knew in a nunnery I could be alone with my books.

""No. I just want to be alone in a cell or someplace where I can figure it all out, Dad."

"Figure what out?" Dad was not happy with our discussion.

"Oh, life, all those things, you know." I was, also, not comfortable with our discussion. But I was determined to be alone some place far away.

My Dad and Mom eventually determined I could go to a college in Europe for just one year but I could not go to Paris—an evil place for a young girl. I got an "A" in French from our French teacher who had been in WW II and was shell-shocked. Boys in the class used to drop a book on the floor from a high place and he would begin to tremble, to lose it. I still feel badly for that "Monsieur," as he insisted we all call him. But I did well in French and had to go to a college where French was spoken. We finally settled on the University of Lausanne in Switzerland. Geneva was "too universal," meaning "too dangerous" for my parent's first child.

When I disembarked from the *Maasdam* in Le Havre, France that August of 1955, I knew immediately I did not KNOW French. With a steamer trunk and two suitcases, I found a taxi (thanks be, it is the same in English and French) which took me to my hotel in Paris. My Dad had booked me there for two nights. Two days later, I would board a train and get myself to Lausanne. In the bathroom of the hotel room in Paris was a little toilet next to the regular toilet. I thought it was a quaint "washing machine." I was washing my undies in it when the hotel clerk knocked on my door to deliver my luggage. "Entrez," I said loudly. When he saw me on my knees in front of the little "toilet," he was appalled and said, "Mademoiselle, c'est un bidet." I had no idea what he was talking about so I just smiled and said, "Oui." "Yes," I found myself saying "oui" all the time to others when I did not understand what they were saying to me.

The train journey from Paris to Lausanne was interesting because so much of the countryside we traveled through was still bombed out—barns and houses with the roofs gone with the wind, forests with all the trees shattered and sharp splinters every where pointing upward, huge bowls of hollow earth, gaping holes looking at the skies. I knew WW II had ended in 1945, but great swaths of rural France were still not revived.

When I arrived in Lausanne, a taxi took me to a neighborhood where there were rooms to rent. When I got into the room, I went out to explore Lausanne. I was so happy to be alone. I felt so FREE.

It was the middle of the afternoon and I was in the middle of the Grand Pont bridge and loving my new city. A pretty girl came up to me and said, "Are you an American?" I said, "Yes, how did you know?" "Oh, I could tell by the way you dress. In Europe we dress different than Americans do." That was true in the 50's. Now almost the whole world dresses like Americans.

I told her my name was Sandy Sweeny and she said her's was Priscilla Schaeffer. She and her family, though Americans, actually lived in Switzerland. We talked for about 20 minutes and she said, "Would you like to come to my family's home for the weekend. We live in a chalet in the mountains." Of course, I would love to come to her chalet in the mountains. She wrote down how I could get to Huemoz. She pronounced Huemoz as Whay-mo. We embraced and I said I'd come up on Friday until Sunday. When we parted, I said to myself, "You're only in Switzerland several hours and you get to go up to Heidi country! What luck!"

When I arrived in Huemoz, Priscilla met me at the curbside where the bus stopped. It was a real trip by train from Lausanne to Aigle and then get a bus ticket a scary up, up to the group of chalets in tiny Huemoz. Chalet les Melezes was the Schaeffer's home. It was a traditional three-story chalet. I had never been in a chalet, but from the outside, it sure looked like Heidi's home in the picture books of my childhood.

Francis, Debby and little Franky met me at the door and were very welcoming. Nice family, I thought. I was taken into the kitchen to meet Priscilla's mother Edith. She was preparing our dinner. Wiping her hand on a kitchen towel, she smiled and embraced me. Then Priscilla took me upstairs to meet her sister Susan who had rheumatic fever and was bed-ridden.

When we sat down to eat the beautiful Chinese dinner Edith had prepared, Francis bowed his head. Oh, they're going to bless the food, I thought. We

L'Abri Chalet

The Schaeffer family when I was there — Fran, Edith, Priscilla, Susan, Debby, Franky

all lowered our heads and father Francis began to pray for many in Switzerland and then he moved on to China and then crossed the Pacific and we came to America (he was still praying) and went all across America and the Atlantic Ocean and finally ended up in Switzerland again. I thought, "Gee, I come 4,000 miles to get away from religious fanatics and the first people I meet are religious fanatics."

In our Junior year, two girls in my crowd had "given their lives to Christ" through a group called Young Life. They were so excited and told me. "Oh, Sandy, you have to give your life to Christ! He's so amazing, etc." Now this innocent enthusiasm did not impress me. I knew the Bible said Jonah was swallowed by a whale and I definitely did not buy that. I argued that none of the Bible can be proven to be true, etc. They took me to their "leader." I asked him about the historicity of the Garden of Eden, about how can a sperm whale swallow a man and then how could he live three days in its belly and not be dead, etc. I had a lot of questions and their "leader" gave me silly answers which told me, "All Christians are stupid people. They don't KNOW anything."

But I was raised well and the Schaeffers were nice people and I was a guest in their home and would not tell them my views on their Christ and thus destroy their faith. I knew life was not meaningful and they were deceived like all believers in any faith were deceived. So I endured the LONG prayer. At dinner my family said real fast "Thank you, dear God, for this our food. Amen."

It was a delicious dinner and I asked Edith how she learned to make such great Chinese food. She said she was born in China and her family had been missionaries there. Missionaries! Definitely totally and absolutely religious people. But very nice people.

As was the Christian and Missionary Alliance-churched Bob, a pimply-faced boy I had had discussions with during lunch hours several months ago in high school. My friends could not understand why I left our lunch table and went to lonely Bob who sat by himself at the other end of the lunch room. Bob was really smart and he was a Christian who took the Bible seriously. He and I went back and forth about real, meaningful things like Jesus as the Son of God and Who was Jesus and why people needed to "KNOW" Him. He lent me a Bible and challenged me to read the four Gospels about Jesus. I went home to my cozy bedroom, read them and the next day gave the Bible back to Bob. He asked me what I thought about Jesus. I did not tell him because I did not want to offend him. But he was, like the Schaeffers, a religious fanatic but a nice person.

After the dinner at the Schaeffers, I began to help Edith and Priscilla clear the table. But Fran said to me, "Let's you and I go downstairs and talk." Edith insisted I do that and we went downstairs and sat near the fireplace.

"So," Francis said, "What are your interests?"

"Archeology, mainly, Mayanology."

"What do you think of the recent Etruscan discoveries?"

Now I had never even heard of or read the word "Etruscan." I was embarrassed. He knew something I didn't know. He began to educate me about them. I was amazed that a religious man high in the mountains knew not only about the Etruscans but about my Mayans. We discussed archeology for a while and I was impressed by what he KNEW.

"What do you think about life and meaning?" he asked as we talked.

"Well," I said, "I'm an existentialist a la Camus not Sartre." My knowledge of the two men was meant to impress him and to sort of shut down any other discussion. I had never encountered people who actually KNEW anything about existentialism.

"Oh, what do you think about Kierkegaard then?" He leaned closer to me.

I had never even heard of that man. Was he an existentialist, also? This Schaeffer man is smart, intelligent and KNEW things I didn't know even though he was religious. He explained Kierkegaard to me. He actually seemed to KNOW what he was talking about.

He quickly jumped away from Kierkegaard and asked me point blank, "Have you considered Christ?"

I had read the four biographies of that man several months previously when Bob had given me that Bible and had come to my own conclusions about him. But in spite of the fact that Schaeffer was smart, I did not want to destroy his faith, so I lied, "He was a good man."

He told me to unpack that phrase "good man."

I have always hated to lie, even fib because fib is just another word for "little lie" and a lie is a lie is a lie. But he just kept pushing me with questions and more questions and probing deeper.

Finally, I said, "Do you want to know who Jesus was?"

He said, "I want to know who you think Jesus was."

He was asking for it. I did not want to hurt him or destroy his faith, but he was asking for it.

"Do you want to know who Jesus really was?" I asked again.

"Yes," he said.

"He was a classic paranoid. He had delusions of grandeur and thought he was God and he had delusions of persecution which gradually got him killed."

That was it. But he had asked for it.

Schaeffer leaned back and laughed. "Who told you this? That's great."

"Nobody told me that. I just read every thing he said about himself: 'I and the father are one;' 'he who has seen me has seen the father, 'I am the resurrection and the life,' 'I am the bread of life,' 'I am the water of life.' People who say this about themselves we lock up in insane asylums, right?"

I don't remember what retort he had to all this. But I was impressed by his KNOWLEDGE. At 18, I thought I was the smart one, but he convinced me in our first discussion that he was smarter than I was. I had never had anyone, except my mother, to share my interests with. I was interested in Schaeffer and wanted to talk more. When I left, I asked if I could come up next weekend. They said, "We'd love to have you come."

I had a friend, Murray, and I took him up with me the next weekend. As Edith would later write of me in Chapter fifteen of her book *L'Abri:* "Sandy... brought a United Nations of people to L'Abri."

The Schaeffers said "L'Abri" in French meant "shelter" and I craved a faraway place where I could further explore Truth with a capital T.

Later, one of the Schaeffers told me that when I left L'Abri that first time, they praised and thanked God because one of their early purposes was "to reach the young wandering around Europe after World War II in the morass of existentialism."

CHAPTER FIFTEEN

God Sends His Choice of People

THIS WAS still the first year of the experiment—or demonstration—of what would happen if we prayed that God would bring the people of His choice, keep others away, send in the needed financial means to care for us all, and open His plan to us. Of course, I cannot list all the people who came, and tell you what happened to each one. But I want you to get some feeling of what really did take place.

There was Sandy, who at first glance might seem just a chattery dizzy little blonde . . . but who really is a "brain". She began to join us for weekends, came to believe, and brought such a variety of people they sounded like the United Nations when listed!

There was Murray, whom we couldn't talk about without calling him "good old Murray". He was the son of a brilliant psychiatrist, with a fine mind himself, and headed for the same profession. He once exclaimed, "What a switch, what a switch. Most students come to Europe with some sort of faith, and go back existentialists. Me, I came with no faith and go back a Bible-believing Christian. . . . What a switch!"

There was Liselotte, a Swiss secretary, boarding in the same *pension* as John, who found she could come to the café discussion group during her lunch hour. She sat by the fireplace one night and said, "Oh I see it *now*. . . ." She did, too, and believed.

First U.S. edition copyright by Edith Schaeffer
Published in 1969 by Tyndale House Publishers

18

CHAPTER 2
STEP INTO THE CIRCLE

Murray was one of my first friends at the University of Lausanne. He was from Indianapolis and was on his Junior Year Abroad from DePaul University. I think ENGLISH was one of the reasons we originally bonded. Both of us were struggling to understand exactly what our teachers were saying and what the students around us were saying. Plus, Murray was a laugher and I love to laugh. When I took him to L'Abri (meaning *"the shelter"*) that next weekend, I told him the Schaeffers were religious but they were nice people and the views from their chalet were unbelievable: "The Dents du Midi are smack in front of you, Murray."

Dents Du Midi – View from L'Abri

Within a month or so of weekend visits to L'Abri, Murray had given his life to Christ. He hung around Edith and she witnessed to him as she did her tasks. I was not pleased that he fell for God/Christ so easily. On the bus and train going back to Lausanne after he had "given his life to Christ," as he said, I tried to tell him that he should be careful about doing that.

I liked, no loved, going up every weekend to the Schaeffers because I loved the conversations with Mr. Schaeffer and the whole "feel" of their home. We called them Mr. and Mrs. Schaeffer for a while and later called her Edith and him Schaeffer. My parents were in their late 40's and the Schaeffers were in their early 40's. L'Abri was for me and for a lot of young people our "second home."

Other people I didn't know would be there, too. Every thing I would posit Schaeffer would answer with Biblical quotes. We would go back and forth for several hours. I would leave on Sundays and go back to my room in Lausanne in Mme. Tschaenan's pensione and get ammunition from my books on how I could refute what he had said. Half of my luggage I took to Europe were clothes and half were my books.

One of those books was a new, small, white leather King James Bible given to me as a Graduation gift from my boyfriend Pete. I knew for sure that Pete's mother had bought that Bible. The reason I took the Bible with me was that several weeks before I left for Europe I had an "experience" with it.

Our beloved half cocker-spaniel dog Teddy was my friend. If something was wrong in my life, I would take him upstairs to my third floor bedroom. I would cry and Teddy would be on my bed with me and I would look into those big brown eyes and know that Teddy was comforting me, understood me. He was my silent best friend. In August two weeks before I left for Europe, Teddy got distemper. I held him close as he trembled and tried to comfort him. He had to be "put down" and I was inconsolable. That night I was crying into my pillow. Even though my mother and father came up to console me, it was useless. Teddy and I would never again cuddle on my bed. Then, suddenly, I realized I had that Bible Pete gave me on my dresser. I got up, opened the book at random, pointed my finger at a verse and read it:

"And every creature which is in heaven, and on the earth, and under the earth, and such as are in the sea, and all that are in them, heard I saying, Blessing, and honour, and glory, and power, be unto him that sitteth upon the throne, and unto the Lamb for ever and ever." Revelation 5:13

I quit crying right away. I said to myself, "So Teddy is in heaven." That was it. I closed the Bible. That little verse had "comforted" me. And that is the reason I took the little white King James Bible with me to the University of Lausanne in Switzerland.

Over the next month or so, I made a lot of friends at the University, We Americans only knew English but most of our new friends knew a little English. We would have fondue dinners together—I had NEVER tasted that most excellent dish. Nor had I ever tasted my German pensione hostess, Madame Tschaenan's, delicious breakfast "cereal" bircher muesli or the chocolate and lemon tarts in the Patisseries or Europe's yogurts with many flavors. When I got back from Europe, I told my Dad he should start a business making flavored yogurts. If he had done that in 1956, he would have made a lot of money.

During our fondue get-togethers, we and our new friends would talk and laugh but they would then translate into English for me and Murray so we would feel included. Even girls from Sweden and Norway understood a lot of French and they spoke English well. I realized how "provincial" we Americans were. But then I thought, that's because we all speak English and have very little contact with people who speak another language. The countries in Europe are small and they are right smack next to each other. They have to know a little of another language because the other language is only 40 miles away from them or right across the border from them. We speak English from state to state and from sea to shining sea and America is one huge country.

I invited lots of these fondue friends up to L'Abri for the weekend— Dutch Justine, three Swedish girls, Helene P. from Norway and many others. Because L'Abri is close to the popular ski resort of Villars or because some had never been up in the Swiss rural mountains, they willingly came. After all, they had free room and board.

In the next two or three months, I, also, invited Muslims, atheists, Buddhists, an animist, unthinking or non-committed people. I took them to L'Abri because I wanted to hear what the Bible and Schaeffer had to say about those religions or ideas. By bringing all those people to L'Abri, I was testing the waters. Could the Bible hold up to my arguments; to the arguments of other religions; where were the weak spots in the Bible; was the Bible just another religious book like the Koran or the Bhagavad Gita; were there really many roads that lead up to the mountain of truth with a capital T, to god with a capital G.?

During the day, most of the ones I brought or who had found their way to Huemoz just hiked, hung around the chalet, made new friends or skied Villars in the winter. Edith always had a breakfast, a lunch and a dinner for us. We loved this *pensione* (in 1955 a rented room in a home or apartment). Edith was a great cook and we did not have to pay a penny for the food, the shelter or the bedding. It was like we were in our own homes. I remember a very handsome young Spanish guy who had been coming to L'Abri on weekends for quite a while. All he did was ski Villars. He would leave in early morning, come back near dark, eat something and then disappear. He never participated in any of our discussions or studies. He was just there freeloading—and the Schaeffers did not seem to mind that.

I did notice in those days, an empty basket on a chair. It was ALWAYS EMPTY. Only when I returned to the States and started getting Edith's newsletter, did I realize it was there in case any of us wanted to put in a franc or two for the weekend. I was appalled at my former ignorance and started to give money regularly to L'Abri in order to "make up" for my and my friends' naivety and ungratefulness. No young person I knew in 1955 or the 6 months into 1956 put a sou in that empty little basket.

Edith told me one afternoon as we were peeling potatoes: "L'Abri is a faith ministry. We don't solicit money. We just pray it in." Pray it in? How does that work? I remember one time after I had given my life to Jesus, Edith and Schaeffer gathered a group of maybe 8 of us together: "We needed $325.19 cents this month and look what happened when we added up the checks from people in America." We all looked at the sheet of paper. There were checks for $25.00 and other monies. When it added up, it came to the EXACT number of $325.19 cents. Edith showed us the last check. The man had written to her: "I just sent the remaining money in my checkbook." That accounted for the 19 cents. I don't remember what number was required that month, but it was the 19 cents that awed me—down to the penny. I live my life like the Schaeffers did at the beginning of L'Abri—on prayer and faith in the Lord to supply our financial and all other needs.

At the beginning, Schaeffer would be teaching and taking questions from the group of about 10 of us downstairs near the fireplace. At first, when he asserted a Biblical quote to a certain question, when I went back to my rented room in an apartment in Lausanne I would say, "How can I refute this?" I would come up the next weekend and give my reasoned rebuttal to what he had said. He would give his Biblical rebuttal to my rebuttal. I did this for about six weeks—"How can I refute this?"

Somewhere along the way, Schaeffer would say something that "made sense" to me and I would go to him and say, "Do you have a book on that subject I can read?" He would give me one of his many books. I would read and study it all week. On the weekend I would go up to Huemoz and tell him, "Thank you for the book. It was helpful."

I do not have a day when I gave my eternity to Christ. My conversion was gradual. I had to be intellectually convinced, to KNOW in my mind that Jesus was Who He claimed to be and that the Bible had Authority.

If one studies the over 300 verses/sections in the Old Testament about the coming *Mashiach* meaning in Hebrew "the anointed one" and then studies the Gospels/biographies of Jesus (Matthew, Mark, Luke and John), it is proof that Jesus of Nazareth fulfilled them all. The New Testament was written in Greek. In Greek the word for "anointed" is *khristós/christos* (Christ). For me, this is/was very persuasive evidence considering that Jesus of Nazareth was born many hundreds of years after those passages were written.

The last hurdle I had to leap over was: Was Jesus' tomb empty? Did He really resurrect from the dead? After all I had learned and studied and underlined in my new, little white Bible, I took the "leap of faith' and said, "YES, He did resurrect from the dead after three days in the tomb as He Himself had prognosticated to His disciples:"

"An evil and adulterous generation craves for a sign; and yet no sign shall be given to it but the sign of Jonah the prophet; for just as Jonah was three days and three nights in the belly of the sea monster, so shall the Son of Man be three days and three nights in the heart of the earth." Matthew 12:39-40

"From that time Jesus began to show to his disciples that he must go to Jerusalem, and suffer many things from the elders and chief priests and scribes, and be killed, and be raised again the third day." Matthew 16:21

"So the Jews answered and said to him, 'What sign do you show to us, since you do these things?' Jesus answered and said to them, 'Destroy this temple, and in three days I will raise it up.' Then the Jews said, 'It has taken forty-six years to build this temple, and will you raise it up in three days?' But he was speaking of the temple of his body. When therefore he was raised from the dead, his disciples remembered that he said this; and they believed the Scripture, and the word which Jesus had spoken." John 2:18-22

"On the next day, which followed the Day of Preparation, the chief priests and Pharisees gathered together to Pilate saying, 'Sir, we remember, while he was still alive, how that deceiver said, "After three days I will rise." Therefore command that the tomb be made secure until the third day, lest his disciples come by night and steal Him away, and say to the people, He has risen from the dead. So the last deception will be worse than the first.'" Matthew 27:62-64

YES, I said, that Great Lion of the Tribe of Judah came roaring out of His tomb just like He said He would—and He's still roaring today.
By mid-October/early November 1955, about two to three months after arriving in Switzerland, I went from saying to myself after Schaeffer's talks: "That's wrong. How can I refute that?" to "That's right. How can I back that up." By that time I was witnessing to all my friends and bringing them and other acquired ones up to L'Abri. I had found TRUTH with a capital T and was excited to tell others and to expose to others the Capital T—TRUTH.
Most people, like my husband Steve, know the exact day and year they became a Christian. I do not know the exact day but the year was 1955. I sort of slipped into the Kingdom. I KNEW I was born-again. I remember a time when Schaeffer, another young man and I were hiking. Schaeffer wore old-

fashioned knickers and heavy wool socks and had a long stick he pushed against as we ascended. He was an eccentric dresser, I thought. Plus Schaeffer did not speak French very well after all his years in the French part of Switzerland and when he spoke French, it was with a casual but heavy, mid-West American accent. Susan and Debby spoke perfect French. I never heard Edith speak anything but English. Sure she knew French but spoke to me/us in English.

On the hike this boy kept telling Schaeffer he did not know if he was a Christian or not. Schaeffer asked him, "Do you believe that Jesus died for your sins?" The boy said, "Yes, I do." "Do you believe Jesus was the Son of God?" "Yes, I do." "Do you believe you are saved by your faith in Him?" "Yes, I do." "Do you know you are a sinner who needs saved?" "Yes, I do." Schaeffer asked several other questions and the answer was always, "Yes, I do." Schaeffer told the boy, "Then you are a Christian." The boy said, "But I don't FEEL like I am a Christian." We stopped walking. Schaeffer took his hiking stick and drew a big circle with it in the dirt. He said to the young man, "Step into this circle and you will be a Christian."

The young man stepped into the circle. He collapsed immediately to the ground and began crying like a baby. Over and over he said, "Thank you, Lord. Thank you, Lord." Schaeffer entered the circle and they embraced as the young man was crying and crying and crying.

To me that was dramatic and I didn't understand what had transpired. And I have wondered off and on over the many decades, "Why did Schaeffer draw that circle? And why did the young man collapse into belief and into crying for joy when he entered the circle? Did he need TO DO something concrete?" Obviously. How did Schaeffer know to do that? Never saw him do any thing like that again the year I was there.

For Christmas break my Norwegian friend Helene whom I brought to L'Abri asked me to come to Murren with her Swedish friends whom I had, also, invited to the Schaeffer's chalet. She and friends were skiers and could hardly wait to ski Murren, but I told her I did not ski. None of the people in Mt. Lebanon at that time took "skiing trips," nor was there even mentions of the word "skiing." Helene knew I ice skated. She told me in Murren they had a beautiful skating rink. So I went with them and paid my share of our huge rented room. Now as I ice skated and did my jumps and twirls on the rink, I would look up at the skiers going easily and gently back and forth, back and forth on the mountain. I said to myself, That looks pretty easy and the third day I rented a pair of skis and went up, up, up in the cable car to the tippy top of the mountain. I had on my black watch plaid wool pants and a sweater under my warm wool jacket.

Someone at the top kindly helped me attach my skis. When I looked down and watched people descend, I noticed there was a sharp left turn you had to make not very far from the "take-off." Seemed if you didn't make that turn, you would go yodeling into the valley below. I, also, noticed that the snow at take-off was not powdery. It was like kernels. Because my current family are skiers, I now know it is called "corn snow." I watched how the skiers pushed off and finally pushed off myself.

The SECOND I pushed off I KNEW I did not KNOW how to ski! But I made that potentially fatal turn by throwing myself to the ground and sliding, butt-down, down the hurtful kernels. When I did that, the whole back of my wool pants ripped off and left a patch of itself on the high ground. I flipped over on my side and awkwardly crawled to a safe place away from the others who were skiing by me and occasionally looking to their left at me.

Now Murren is considered one of the longest ski trails in the world. It is 9.8 miles long (15.8 kilometers). It took me about 6 hours to reach the bottom. I would get up, ski close to the ground with my bloody behind showing (I could have cared less!) and then fall and crawl myself out of the way. Eventually I noticed that some boys would stop when I stopped. I would say, "Passez, s'il vous plait." They replied, "Non, mademoiselle, apres vous." ("Pass, please. No, mademoiselle, after you.")

Finally in late afternoon when I got to the top of the place where I could see clear sailing all the way to a little shop at the bottom, I determined to ski to it in one fell swoop. I kept going faster and faster and didn't know HOW I was going to stop. The closer I got, I heard an older man with a Meerschaum pipe yelling at me, "Schtem! Schtem! Schtem!" I knew he was trying to help an out-of-control me but I had no idea what he was saying. The SHORT of it was: I threw myself to the ground and had the bruises to prove it—in addition to the bloody behind. That night in Murren, no matter where we all went, my skiing descent and landing were "the topics."

I had another experience during that "skiing vacation"—an oxymoron to me. (I have NEVER been on skis since that time even though my family are ardent skiers.) I decided to take the little train from Murren and then go down to Lauterbrunnen for the day. Murren has no cars so one cannot drive to or from Murren. I took the first train in the early morning to the cable car where I would descend to Lauterbrunnen. Only the driver and I were in that one-car little train. Suddenly, the car skipped the tracks! To make a long story short, the conductor found a fallen medium-sized tree for a lever. He (mostly he) and I put the tree under the locomotive and put the wheel back on its track. As Archimedes, that most intelligent of men, said about levers: "Give me a place to stand and I will move the earth."

In Lauterbrunnen I met some American GI's stationed in Germany. I told them my conversion story and told them about our Lord. I said if they could ever get to L'Abri, they should go. They were two Jims and a Peter or Paul. Hope those guys went to L'Abri.

After I had become a Christian, I took as my life verse Romans 1:16: "For I am not ashamed of the gospel of Christ: for it is the power of God unto salvation to every one that believeth; to the Jew first, and also to the Greek." One never knows what happens to strangers we meet and witness to about our God. But one always knows we are to cast our Bread upon the waters and God will determine the outcome. As the evangelist Edith would say, "There is no accidental meeting. It is always a providential meeting." And I live that proverb on planes, trains and on the streets of America and Europe. A Christian friend of ours in Connecticut, Lee Buck (now deceased), was a traveling businessman who always made it a point to witness to the person sitting next to him on a plane. On one of his plane rides in the 1970's he met a woman named Margaret Mead. He told her the whole Gospel story and asked her to commit her life to Christ. Even though she had listened with rapt attention, she declined. Lee gave her his card and went on his merry way and she hers. He had no idea he had witnessed to the famous Margaret Mead, the academic and anthropologist who was known in most circles as a cutting-edge anthropologist ever since she wrote a book in 1928 called *Coming of Age in Samoa*. Several years later, a woman knocked on the door of Lee's home in Connecticut. When he answered the door, a woman was standing there who said she had a message for him from Margaret Mead. He vaguely remembered, but invited her in. She had lived with Margaret Mead for many decades and Mead had told this woman about the man on the plane. As Mead was dying, she gave Lee's card to her and said, "Go to this man after I am dead and tell him I did what he asked me to do."
So maybe Margaret Mead did commit her life to Christ—only she and He know. "Chance meetings" do, as Edith firmly believed, often turn into "divine appointments."
At the very beginning of L'Abri a handsome American boy named John Sandri was there. I don't know how he originally came to Huemoz or when exactly he came to faith in the Lord. But John's original faith was labored into him through Francis Schaeffer. When we talked, I found out John was from Scarsdale, New York. Murray and I immediately made an American connection to John. I think he had Swiss parents who lived in Scarsdale, New York. Maybe Priscilla who was the point girl for L'Abri at the University and had invited many students to L'Abri had brought John to L'Abri?
I knew Priscilla really "liked" John. When Murray and I left L'Abri to go back home in 1956, I had a talk with John and told him Priscilla was "really fond, was maybe in love with you, John." Suggested to him that he and Priscilla might get married. He was a little startled by that. "Oh, maybe not," he said. They did end up married, had children and are still living in a chalet in Huemoz near Chalet les Melezes where it all began.

CHAPTER 3
BRAIN & SOUL

By late October, many people were coming to L'Abri. The "regulars" like I was did not even know them. How they found their way to Huemoz I do not know. The Schaeffers had friends in England and a Hans Rookmaaker in Holland whom Schaeffer really admired had been his friend for years. I think he was a professor in Art somewhere in Holland? (Perhaps that friendship sparked Schaeffer's later intense interest in all the Arts?) The name Rookmaaker was a big name when I was there. The Schaeffers began to go to Milan, Italy once in a while and then weekly to teach Bible classes. Maybe some of these contacts had sent these people, I thought. A diligent Worker, Dorothy Jamieson, (I think Dorothy was the first to be called a "Worker") had come to help Edith with the many tasks she had entertaining, cooking, changing beds and all the growing requirements at Chalet les Melezes.
"Meleze" is the French name for what we call in English the "Larch tree." I was not aware of trees and their names or of flowers and their names until many decades later when I embarked upon my Gardens and Herbs years. Don't know if there were aromatic Larch trees in and around Chalet les Melezes. There apparently were or why would they name the chalet Chalet les Melezes, "alpine cottage (amidst) the Larch trees."

L'Abri Les Melezes ("larch trees")

But there were always vegetable gardens at L'Abri which Edith and others had planted in the Spring and we ate wonderful fresh and preserved dinners from those gardens in the Fall and Winter.

The Schaeffers made a Prayer List of people and things we could, should pray about. Later, those of us who were new Christians or regular visitors would covenant to pray for certain needs/people for one hour. The list was posted with the hours and we could sign up if we wished. I am a night owl so I would take the 10:00 o'clock to 11:00 hour when most were asleep. In the beginning, whole days and their hours were bathed in prayer for the Work at L'Abri.

Susan, in bed upstairs with rheumatic fever, was on the top of the List. She was an amazing young girl. She had taught herself Braille and exchanged letters with young people all over the world who were blind or almost blind. It was her "ministry." She resembled Schaeffer's features and was sandy-haired rather than her dark-haired mother and two sisters. The whole time I was there, I never saw a sad look on Susan's face or never heard a complaining word from her mouth. She was to me at the time a Godly witness to victory over disease. She didn't just endure, she overcame. She redeemed what was a bad thing. Every time I went to Huemoz I would go upstairs to her and she would be up-beat and talkative. We were so thankful to God when she and her parents returned home from a doctor's visit in the Spring of 1956 and she had been totally healed!! Bathed and cleansed in hours of prayer by many people.

The Schaeffers would pray, "Lord, bring the people of Your choice and keep all others away." I thought it was sort of strange, that part about "keep all others away." But after decades of ministry, I have seen the truth of "keeping all others away." Because all the "others" could be sent or be coming to disturb a ministry and not to explore or to understand Biblical TRUTH. I've wasted a lot of valuable time answering questions from people who are not processing the answers or are just wondering what I would say or are just shooting the breeze. Then they go away and I pray for their salvation. But I, also, have learned: "A man convinced against his will is of the same opinion still."

I never heard Schaeffer tell the story of the founding of L'Abri. But Edith was fond of telling how L'Abri came to be. In fact, I've since thought that L'Abri and the whole ministry was shaped and envisioned by that China Inland Mission woman. Schaeffer was the "brain" of L'Abri and Edith was the "soul" of L'Abri.

She first told me the story in the kitchen while we were preparing something for a dinner. She would stop the story, look at me and say, "God is amazing, Sandy, isn't He?" According to my memory and after so many decades it may not be exactly how it all happened, but here is what I remember hearing as an 18 year-old new convert to Christ:

Schaeffer was the "brain" of L'Abri and Edith was the "soul"

The Schaeffer family had initially gone to Europe under the auspices of a group called Children for Christ. In America Schaefer had been a minister somewhere and there had been some kind of "serious break" between his theology and those friends whom he had thought had his same views about the Bible and God. They had become "liberal," a word which was a bad word then.

As I remember Edith's story of the founding of L'Abri, they were summarily "kicked out" of Champery where they lived because they were making converts to Christ in the Catholic canton of Valais. (A canton in Switzerland is like a state in America.) Edith always emphasized that a Mr. Ex (maybe his name was Mr. Exupery?) who was an important man in that canton had been led to Christ. That was enough for the "powers that be" in the canton. The Schaeffers were to leave in a very short time but they had no place to go. They prayed and prayed and finally on a snow-banked day in Huemoz she found a chalet. She fell on her knees into the snow and thanked God for leading her to just that place. But they had no money to buy Chalet les Melezes in the canton of Vaud. They prayed and the money to buy the chalet miraculously came in from people in America (maybe?). I was very inspired by that story and particularly by the miracles which were the result of PRAYER. "Prayer Affects MATTER" is what I always say.

The name "Covenant Seminary" was, also, mentioned by Schaeffer with fondness. In spite of that, he said several times, "Get out of the seminaries and get into journalism." I always thought Schaeffer was one of the Founders of Covenant, but am now disabused of that. But Covenant Seminary, founded in 1956, does have a Francis Schaeffer Institute so his "true truth" was influential there at that time.

I remember Schaeffer occasionally railed against the World Council of Churches. Of course, I had no idea what that organization was and had no idea why Schaefer had such vitriol against them. But if Schaeffer thought it was bad, it was probably bad. He often railed against "liberal" theology" that he said had crept into the Church. Now I was not raised in the Church. My family was what our pastor son calls "Chreesters" (people who only go to church on Christmas and Easter). So at that time I had no idea what Schaeffer was talking about, but because he was my mentor, I knew liberal theology must be bad. I know now what Schaeffer was talking about and totally agree that unless all theological assumptions and assertions are based on the Bible (*sola scriptura*) as the inerrant Word of God to man, they are not espousing original/historical Christianity but are just the sound and the fury signifying nothing. I have no concrete idea if the World Council of Churches' beliefs or his erstwhile friends changing beliefs precipitated not only the Schaeffer's eventual journey to Switzerland but the later "spiritual crisis" for Fran.

Perhaps leading up to and during Schaeffer's spiritual crisis, he experienced not just anguish but anger. I saw him annoyed/angry several times. The most striking illustration of anger was: a famous Christian man from England (so wish I could recall WHO he was) had come to L'Abri to meet with Schaeffer. The man, Schaeffer and about 8 of us were on the lawn in front of Chalet les Melezes. We, as bystanders, were not a part of their "discussion." They exchanged a few pleasantries. Then their discussion about doctrines, I think it was, became contentious. They went back and forth. I could see that my mentor was getting really angry. The other man was adamant but not angry. Their exchange went on for maybe half an hour or so. Schaeffer then said he was leaving. The other man said, "Let's pray about this" and put out his hands. Schaeffer said to him point blank, "We don't pray to the same God" and walked away leaving the man and us just standing there, ASTOUNDED. After I had returned from Switzerland, my Mother and sister saw on TV an exchange between Schaeffer and another man. They both said to me that Schaeffer did not come off well because he was very contentious. I told them he was probably debating with a man who was either not a Christian or who was not speaking Biblically. They were convinced he was an "angry man." I had seen close-up that side of Francis Schaeffer several times.

Another instance of his anger was with Franky. Franky was a real presence at that time in the household. We all doted on him. But he often did "bad boy" things, as three-year-olds do. He had disobeyed or done a "bad boy" thing that particular day and Schaeffer was mad. But he said, "I'm furious now, Franky, but I will wait until this evening to punish you and then I will not be angry." I thought that was a great way to treat one's anger with children. Later in the afternoon, Schaeffer called to Franky and spanked him. I loved how he controlled himself that way. I respected that. My many spankings as a "bad girl" were immediately delivered over my father's lap with his hand or a thin, wooden slat.

When I was at L'Abri, Franky was a 3-year-old who had had polio and still limped in one leg. He and I used to play a "hanging game" where I would hang his limp leg on a door knob and we would laugh (inexplicable to me now). Franky was very active and smart. I really loved him during the time I spent in L'Abri. He was the youngest member of L'Abri and everyone paid a lot of attention to him and not because he had a limp but because he was vibrant and interesting. He looked like his father as did Susan. Franky never had a "play date" with anyone his own age, but he was blessed to have the attention of all of us at that early time in his life.

Edith said Fran had a recent period in his life where he had to rethink his whole theology and beliefs. He would be upstairs (maybe in their chalet in Champery, Switzerland?) struggling and re-reading the Bible and she knew he was in deep trouble with his faith. She told me, "Fran would be agonizing upstairs above me and I would be under him praying to and petitioning God to bring him back to faith in Christ." When Schaeffer came out of his doubting period, he was stronger and more convinced of his faith and of the Truths in the Bible than ever before. Edith looked on that period as preparation for the Work that was ahead of him at L'Abri. I was shocked this intelligent and earnest man had ever doubted his faith in the Bible and Christ that he so convincingly taught to us. But Edith said the Lord was forming him into the man he had to be in order to do the work he had to do.

Schaeffer's period of faith crisis

So God had turned a bad thing into a good thing. Jesus is Redeemer. "To redeem" means to "retrieve, regain, recover, get back, reclaim, repossess, rescue." Without Schaeffer's period of doubt and the "regaining/recovering" of his faith in Christ and the Bible, he probably would not have become one the greatest apologists for the faith in the latter part of the 20th century. In my life there have been periods or incidents when I wondered where God was in all this. I would remember God's victory in Schaeffer's life and I especially remember the power of God flowing through Edith's faithful prayers to her Lord and Savior for her distressed husband.

Recently when our son-in-law suddenly died of SADS (Sudden Arrhythmia Death Syndrome) on a ski slope in Utah, the first thing I said to our bereft daughter was, "We have a big pile of shit in front of us, Kathy. I can't wait to see the beautiful garden the Lord will plant on this." Manure is, of course, the best fertilizer. And many symbolic as well as an actual "garden dedicated to Walt DeTour" have come out of our precious Walt's death. A good thing out of a bad thing. ONLY our GOD can make that happen, can redeem any thing or one.

Edith told me one time that L'Abri had a board of Directors. That sounded very official to me. She said her father, George Seville, and the man from Valais, (Mr. Ex,) and she and Francis were the Board of Directors. I wondered WHY did they need a Board of Directors, but Edith seemed to be happy they had one, so I was, too.

Schaeffer referred to his conversion story from time to time as he talked to us. Here is what remains in my 18 year-old mind about that. Schaeffer had a "difficult" upbringing and was always a seeker after the truths about all this living on earth. He read the Bible from the beginning to the end when he was a young man and believed it. Then one day he entered a church or tent meeting where there was an evangelist called Anthony Zeoli preaching salvation. When Zeoli gave an altar call, Schaeffer went up and gave his life to Christ. He was converted.

NOW—I know one of God's beautiful ironies. Francis Schaeffer was born in 1912 and was 20 years old when the evangelist Anthony Zeoli's son, Billy, was born in 1932. Francis and Billy 'found" each other in the 1970's. By that time, Billy Zeoli was a successful business man and Francis Schaeffer was a known apologist for the Christian faith. Billy introduced Schaeffer and his son Franky (now known as Frank) to wealthy American evangelical business men like Amway's Richard DeVos. These Christian entrepreneurs financed the 1977 successful documentary film series *How Should We Then Live: The Rise and Decline of Western Thought and Culture*. That popular series galvanized many evangelicals Against Abortion. The United States Supreme Court ruling *Roe Versus Wade* in 1973 condoning "a woman's right to have an abortion" was immediately opposed by the Roman Catholic Church. (When I picketed Against Abortion in Danbury, Ct and Naples, Fl as late as the 1990's, it was always me and the Catholics.) So it took a long time for the Protestant Evangelical Community to wake up. But the Schaeffers' documentary was the underpinnings of the current strong opposition to abortion by both Catholics, Protestants and sane people. Anthony Zeoli brought Francis Schaeffer to Salvation and Anthony's son, Billy Zeoli, brought financial backers to Schaeffer for his film series which has been the SALVATION of many, many, little, tiny lives.

At L'Abri in 1955-56, Schaeffer railed against "the decline of Western Civilization." He would explain to us how the Wellhausen School of Higher Criticism in Germany in the late 1880's started the ball rolling down the hill. He said Wellhausen was the first "scholar" who stated that the Torah, the first five books in the Old Testament, was NOT written by Moses but was a compilation of many sources that were written over many hundreds of years. And his School of Higher Criticism was/is taken seriously. This *a priori,* unverified assumption was the first academic attack upon modern Christian Western culture. And it was aimed at the Bible's claim that it was the Word of God. What a clever strategy Wellhausen had—Hit the foundational beliefs of the West. All our morals, beliefs and laws were founded on the Bible—at that time.

When I came back from Europe in 1956, I enrolled at the University of Pittsburgh. In an English class we read *Huckleberry Finn* by Mark Twain, that wonderful, beloved-by-children story of the adventures of teenage Huck and his young, black friend Jim. The professor stated the relationship of the two young boys was really a homosexual relationship. Having read the book as a child and then again in college, I protested. The teacher referred me to an article by Leslie Fieldler "Come Back to the Raft Ag'in, Huck Honey!" that demonstrated this homosexual theme. In fact, this Fiedler claimed homosexuality was a recurrent theme in American literature which had been "overlooked." I was astonished a simple relationship between a white boy and a black boy could be twisted to imply a homosexual relationship. There was NOTHING in Twain's text that had a shred of evidence of that. Like there was not a shred of evidence given by Wellhausen that Moses was not the author of the Torah. The West in its decline now believes any thing an "authority" in a profession states. Often the original hypothesis goes from a theory to a truth which most assume is true. Francis Schaeffer taught me to examine thoroughly, to be a critical thinker, to look always for "true truth," as he called it. Otherwise we fall and become members of the Fall.

I have a wooden plaque with a saying painted on it hanging over my front door in Vermont.

"TRUTH IS NOT ALWAYS POPULAR BUT IT IS ALWAYS TRUE"

CHAPTER 4
CAFÉ DU VIEUX

In November of 1955 so many people were coming to L'Abri from the University of Lausanne that we started meeting for Bible Study once a week in Lausanne in a Cafe near the University, the Cafe du Vieux.

At first there was only Murray, me, several of my Swedish friends and Priscilla and John. But week by week there were many more coming. That was great but it was tedious for the original group because if there was even one new person, Schaeffer insisted we start at the very beginning of the Study for the new one or ones. He had given us a study of the Bible mimeographed on white paper and stapled together. All my notes were on the page we were studying, so as a new one or ones came, I had to start at the very first page again even though some of us were really on the e.g. 5th page. It was frustrating for the original group. In hindsight, however, it was probably good for us to have all those Bible verses and explanations drilled into us.

On reflection, I wonder whether the owner of the Cafe knew we were doing a Bible Study. He had to have known because I think it was Schaeffer who asked him if we could be there in the Cafe near the University steps once a week. We were in an alcove of the cafe and could hear the rattling of dishes, the murmurs of talking customers, the scraping of chairs and the smell of good food. But none of us bought any thing to eat when we were there, so we were not "increasing the owner's profits." Maybe he was a Christian or was just sympathetic to why we were there. God bless him.

When I returned to Lausanne in 1971 with my husband Steve, I was anxious to show him not only L'Abri but the Cafe du Vieux in Lausanne where we met for Bible Studies. When we went there, there it was!

Cafe du Vieux

We went in and I showed him the side room where we gathered together. The Cafe was still thriving and filled with people! I was so happy to be there and to show Steve where we met by the steps leading up to the University of Lausanne. But much to my total surprise, "they" had moved the University way out of town. When we went out there, we found a bunch of pre-fab buildings hastily scattered together! BUT the Cafe, now called Vieux-Lausanne had lasted and is still thriving! Thank God for immutability!

We all brought bag lunches to the Cafe. Mme Tschannen from whom I rented a bedroom packed me a delicious ham sandwich on a buttered hard roll. Believe it or not, I had NEVER had bread with hard crusts. I had had only store-bought bread with soft crusts. Everyone I knew in Mt. Lebanon at that time ate Wonder Bread. The first time I had Europe's delicious bread, I fell in love with it. I can still get that same "jambon sandwich" in Luc's Cafe in Ridgefield, Connecticut. When I am eating it, it always reminds me of the crowded group around the increasingly large circle in the Cafe du Vieux with Schaeffer in the middle of us with his Bible-study stapled papers and all of us around him with our stapled papers learning and questioning and learning again and again the Words of God.

At the beginning in his teachings, Schaeffer emphasized over and over again how Christ died for our sins "ONCE AND FOR ALL." He always pronounced a Greek word after he had said "ounce and for all" that sounded to me like "epifa." I didn't know Greek then but in college at the University of Pittsburgh I was offered a Classics Scholarship so I ended up taking three years of Greek—just enough to haltingly read the New Testament in Koine Greek.

Christ's death "once and for all" was very important to Schaeffer. It meant that Christ's death on the Cross for SIN (yours, mine, everyone's sins) was the final and only way for one's sins to be atoned for. No more blood sacrifices or other ways up the mountain, so to speak. Christ did it ALL on the Cross and His final words, "It is finished," meant He DID what He was born TO DO.

In Greek the word for "once and for all" is *ephapax* pronounced "efapax," an adverb meaning "once for all." The proof texts for this comes from:

Hebrews 7:27 "Unlike the other high priests, he does not need to offer sacrifices day after day, first for his own sins, and then for the sins of the people. He sacrificed for their sins once for all when he offered himself."

I Peter 3:18 "For indeed Christ died for sins once for all, the Just and Righteous for the unjust and unrighteous the Innocent or the guilty so that He might bring us to God, having been put to death in the flesh, but made alive in the Spirit."

I had sort of fixated on that strange word because he used the Greek word right after he had said that "Christ dealt with your sin, my sin, all sin, once and for all, *efapax,* on the Cross." And he taught: "Christ atoned for our sin ONCE on the Cross and there is no remission of our sins except that and that was only Once For All (*efapax*) when he went to the Cross."

Schaeffer, also, emphasized to us Christ as Prophet, Priest and King. Jesus of Nazareth was the One prophesied centuries ago by the Hebrew prophets in the Old Testament—the *Mashiach/Messiah* in Hebrew/Greek. Moses starting in c. 1400's BC had prophesied Jesus:

"I will raise up for them a prophet like you from among their fellow Israelites, and I will put my words in his mouth. He will tell them everything I command him. I myself will call to account anyone who does not listen to my words that the prophet speaks in my name." Deuteronomy 18:18,19

Jesus was the prophesied Prophet Himself. Before His death, He, as a Prophet, prophesied the Destruction of Jerusalem and in the Revelation to John by Jesus after His Ascension, He prophesied much that would happen before He returns again.

For me the Old Testament prophecies of Jesus and the New Testament fulfillments were one of the main things that brought my mind to Christ. There are over 300 prophecies of the coming Messiah in the Old Testament, all written hundreds of years before Jesus of Nazareth was even born. And the Dead Sea Scrolls had been discovered and proved these Before Christ (BC) ancient prophecies were right there and had not been "inserted by well-meaning monks," as some so-called scholars had asserted. The math says that the chances of one man fulfilling all those BC prophesies is 1 chance in 10 to the 157th power. That was high enough for non-mathematical me. Jesus WAS the long-prophesied One.

The High Priests in the Old Testament, and even when Jesus was alive, interceded for the sins of the Jews by once every year releasing into the desert a scapegoat carrying with it the sins of all the people for that year. (Leviticus 16:20-22) But Christ as our High Priest entered only once into the Holy of Holies and took care of our sins Forever—not just for a year.

As King, Jesus is Ruler, Regulator and Redeemer, the highest of highest, the greatest of the great and He is, also, Lord: "On his robe and on his thigh he has this name written: KING OF KINGS AND LORD OF LORDS." (Revelation 19:16) He rules in the Kingdom of Heaven and over the kingdoms of this earth.

Jesus as Prophet, Priest and King were drilled into me by Schaeffer.

Schaeffer had an interesting take on Baptism. After I had given my life to Christ, I asked him one day as we were on a hike (he loved to hike—and to talk during hikes). "Should I be baptized now that I am a true Christian?" He asked me, "Were you ever baptized?" I explained to him when my brother Johnny, 5 years younger than I, was born, my father thought we three children should be baptized. We all dressed up and baby Johnny was in a long white dress. It was not a public baptism. We were at the doors at the back of the empty Episcopal Church in Warren, Ohio—the minister, my father, my mother, my sister, my baby brother and I were the only ones there. The minister first sprinkled water over my head, then my sister's head and then took Johnny into his arms and said the same words he said to my sister and me and sprinkled water over his little head. I did not feel any different. Schaeffer said I was a believer now and had already been baptized. He would baptize me if I wanted, but there was no reason for doing it again.

But I did feel something different when I was 12 and went to a church with my friend and her family. I can still see the small church in Alliance, Ohio on a tree-lined street dotted with nice brick homes. I don't remember how many times I went to the church on Sunday with my friend and her family, but it was probably often. My mother said to me one day, "The minister of the church where you have gone with your friend Judy called me today and told me you wanted to be confirmed along with all the other children. He asked my permission to confirm you. I told him if you had expressed interest in being confirmed, I give my permission." I don't remember asking the minister if I could be confirmed. I did not even know what that word meant. But I told Mother I did want to be with all those other children the next Sunday. She bought me a pretty new white dress.

I don't remember going that Sunday, but I do have a firm and absolute memory of what happened. We all knelt on a cushion in front of the altar. I was in the middle of the line of children. The minister started to the left of me, said some things and then did something to each forehead. When he came to me, I don't remember what he said, but he put his thumb on my forehead and said something and then moved on. When he put his thumb on my forehead, he made a sign that I thought was an X. The second he did that, my forehead where the sign was became very hot as though he had burned my forehead. I wanted to rub that place but didn't because none of the other children had done that.

I asked Judy if she felt like her forehead was burned when he touched it. She said, "No, he was only making the sign of the Cross, Sandy." Even though I was 12 when that happened, today, decades later, I feel that faint warmth of the Cross when I remember that experience. I now know God was sealing me even though I did not give my life to Christ until I was 18.

Several times Schaeffer was talking near the fireplace and there were maybe 25 people there questioning him and him giving answers. I was in a folding chair on the first row. It was late into the evening and he had been talking for several hours. I looked over at him and his eyes were closed. It seemed he was asleep and maybe he was, but he just kept talking Biblical sense. I saw that maybe 2-3 times and have told others about that. I am still amazed that even dog-tired, half-asleep Schaeffer could answer questions cogently.

Schaeffer said something I have always remembered and repeated to others over my decades as a Christian—"The universe obeys God by natural law. Animals obey God through natural instinct. Only man obeys God through Choice/his Will."

One afternoon when snow was slowly falling and we were all around Schaeffer near the fireplace, he casually said, "We can never know God COMPLETELY but we can know Him TRULY." He continued speaking.

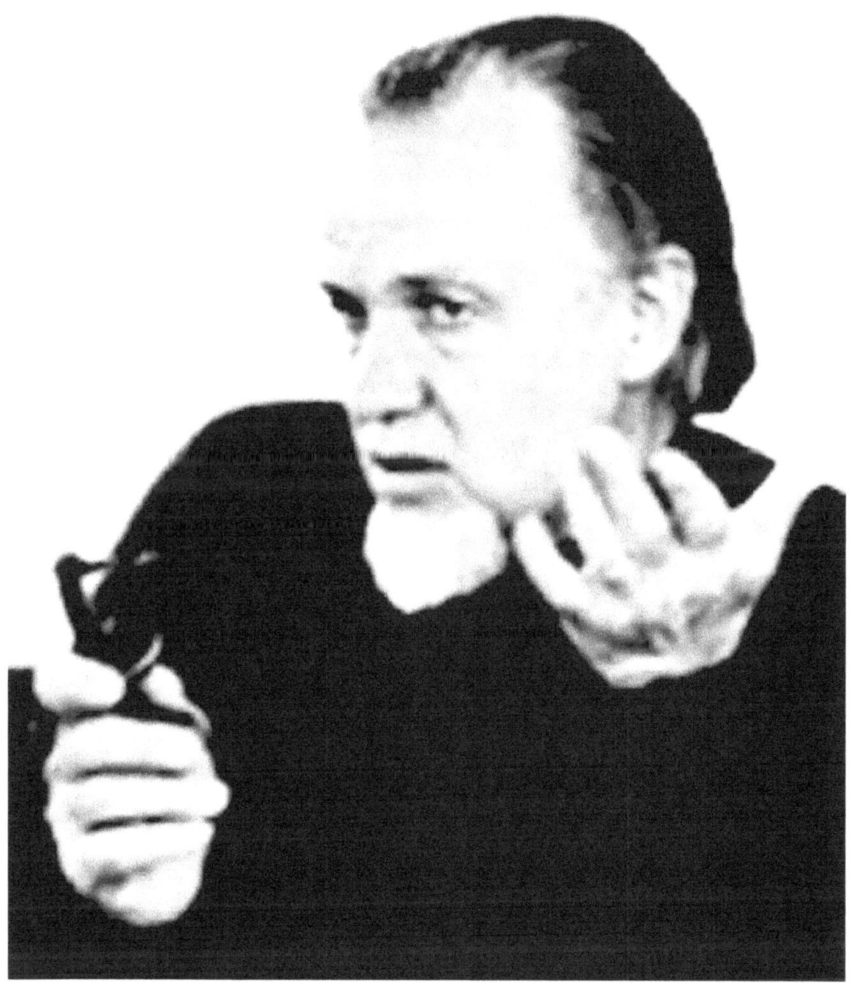

That ad lib profound statement has forever been embedded in my mind. At my time at L'Abri Schaeffer taught that Melchizedek in the Old Testament was not only a "type" of Christ but was Christ Himself in manifestation as the book of Hebrews in the New Testament seems to be saying:

"This Melchizedek was king of Salem and priest of God Most High. He met Abraham returning from the defeat of the kings and blessed him, and Abraham gave him a tenth of everything (a tithe). First, the name Melchizedek means 'king of righteousness'; then also, 'king of Salem' means 'king of peace. Without father or mother, without genealogy, without beginning of days or end of life, resembling the Son of God, he remains a priest forever." Hebrews 7:1-3 NIV

We are introduced to the mysterious Melchizedek in Genesis 14:18:

"Then Melchizedek king of Salem brought out bread and wine (to Abram).
He was priest of God Most High, and he blessed Abram, saying,
'Blessed be Abram by God Most High,
   Creator of heaven and earth.
And praise be to God Most High,
   who delivered your enemies into your hand.'
Then Abram gave him a tenth of everything." Genesis 14:18-20 NIV

There are many theories about this Melchizedek. Schaeffers's theory is as good as any, I think. Certainly Jesus as High Priest offered the ultimate sacrifice—Himself. During the time when Jesus was living, one of the High Priests was Ishmael Ben Phabi (15,16 AD) and the Jews confess that "after the death of Ishmael Ben Phadi, the splendour of the priesthood ceased." Perhaps Jesus' Self-Sacrifice as our High Priest annulled all other Jewish sacrifices?
Schaeffer, also, taught: "When Man fell in the Garden of Eden (and Schaeffer believed and I believe in the historicity of Bible "stories"), Man fell away from God; Man fell away from Man and Man fell away from Nature." A trinity of Falls.
Schaeffer said several times what it means for Man to be "like" God Who breathed Himself into our nostrils. (Genesis 2:7) Schaeffer said we are like God in that: "we think; we act and we feel."
I've never heard or read others put forth Schaeffer's meaning of the word *ABBA*. He believed it meant the very endearing word "DADDY." *Ab* is in Hebrew "father" but think his meaning of the word is like saying, "*AB,AB*," a very young Hebrew child's way of saying "Daddy." In Gethsemane Jesus was really overwhelmed and cried out to His Father/His Daddy:

"He took Peter, James and John along with him, and he began to be deeply distressed and troubled. 'My soul is overwhelmed with sorrow to the point of death,' he said to them. 'Stay here and keep watch.' Going a little farther, he fell to the ground and prayed that if possible the hour might pass from him. 'Abba, Father,' he said, 'everything is possible for you. Take this cup from me. Yet not what I will, but what you will.'" Mark 8:33-36

CHAPTER 5
TRUE TRUTHS

The time came in the late Spring of 1956 when Murray and I were leaving in several weeks for home. Schaeffer wanted to have a special "going-away teaching" for us since we had been there at the beginning. We went up for the weekend. On a sunny, Alpine late Spring morning, Edith had Pricilla, John, Murray, me and Schaeffer arranged at a little table on the outside balcony facing the Dents du Midi. Schaeffer began by pointing to the hillside across the road and said, "This is the first meeting of Farel House."
I had no idea who or what he was talking about. He explained to us that William Farel was a Protestant reformer a long time ago right there in the Canton of Vaud where L'Abri was. I assumed Schaeffer was identifying with that Farel.
Sometime in the late 50's/early 60's a Farel House was built right where Schaeffer had pointed—across the road on a sloping hill. It became an integral part of their ministry.

Farel House

As the years after 1956 rolled by, Schaeffer recorded lots of tapes on lots of Biblical and other subjects and students crossed the narrow road, went down the hill, entered Farel House and listened to and discussed them. Farel House's Library included many books by Christian authors like Lucado and Yancey, but Nietzche and Richard Dawkins books were there, too. One HAS to know opposing views, you know.
But back to what Schaeffer called "the first meeting of Farel House." Edith, of course, brought us tea and goodies, always in all ways the supreme hostess.

Schaeffer had us open our Bibles to Philippians 4:4-9. In my small, white King James Bible it read:

"Rejoice in the Lord always: and again I say, Rejoice.
Let your moderation be known unto all men. The Lord is at hand.
Be careful for nothing; but in every thing by prayer and supplication with thanksgiving let your requests be made known unto God.
And the peace of God, which passeth all understanding, shall keep your hearts and minds through Christ Jesus.
Finally, brethren, whatsoever things are true, whatsoever things are honest, whatsoever things are just, whatsoever things are pure, whatsoever things are lovely, whatsoever things are of good report; if there be any virtue, and if there be any praise, think on these things.
Those things, which ye have both learned, and received, and heard, and seen in me, do: and the God of peace shall be with you."

I remember thinking and still think the last verse in Philippians 4:9 when Paul says "received, and heard, and seen in me, do," Schaeffer was substituting "me" (Paul) for himself (Francis Schaeffer). To this day, I cannot think of one thing Francis or Edith Schaeffer taught me at the Beginning of L'Abri that I, born-again, evangelist and daily researching the Old and New Testaments, do not believe was "true truth" (as Schaeffer used to call it) or as I always call it Truth with a capital T.

Once three or so decades ago I made for my three children a little embroidered and very messy piece of white cotton with the words from Philippians 4:8:

"Finally, brethren, whatever things are true, whatever things are noble, whatever things are just, whatever things are pure, whatever things are lovely, whatever things are of good report, if there is any virtue and if there is anything praiseworthy—meditate on these things."

I know that some at that small table on the sunny deck at L'Abri as our goodbye lesson was being taught in the Spring of 1956 fell away from the faith and others have abandoned the Truths Schaeffer instilled in us. Many other Schaeffer-ites have criticized and censured the Schaeffers as well as L'Abri.

But I can attest that after many decades in the Lord, I have "the God of Peace with me" for which I am grateful with all my heart to Francis and Edith Schaeffer who gave their lives and love and Godly words and behaviors to me at L'Abri at the Beginning.

CHAPTER 6

After
The Beginning of L'Abri

I went back to the United States on the *Liberte*. As I sat on the deck watching the wonders of the waters of the Atlantic, I kept thinking, "I'm the only one in the Unites States who is a Christian in the real meaning of that word." I was, it must be stated, still 18. The Young Life Christians and the Missionary Alliance Christian I knew in high school had been totally erased from my mind by that year at L'Abri. I felt it was my duty and, yes, privilege to bring the Gospel to the States. As I type those words, it is embarrassing and shows how naive I was at that time. Schaeffer and Edith and the people coming to the Lord at L'Abri were real Christians and that is what I was thinking as I sailed the seas home.

When my family picked me up in Hoboken, they saw I had gained some weight in Europe. I started out weighing 110 lbs and ended up weighing 135 lbs. I blamed the crusty bread in Europe and the Patisseries where I daily got either chocolate or lemon tarts. Plus in the *pensione* for breakfast I had a bowl of *bircher muesli* (wonderful rolled oats with dried or fresh fruits in it); then a big meal for lunch (which over there was like a dinner) and a meal for dinner (which is like our lunch). Within 6 weeks in the USA, I weighed 110 lbs again because I reverted to my normal eating habits: no breakfast; occasional lunch; dabbled at dinner. But when my younger sister Carol called Tooie, age 16, first saw me get off the boat and walk up to them she said, "I feel like a wand."

My father's reaction to my conversion was: "Jesus Christ, I send you to Europe and you come home a Communist!"

"But, Daddy, I'm not a Communist, I'm a Christian."

My Mother's reaction was: "I'm sure you've had a wonderful time in Switzerland, honey, and have discovered new things."

"No, Mom, I have given my life to Christ. I'm a Christian."

I talked to my brother Johnny many times about the Lord. He, then 13, was very open to the Lord and gave his life to Christ when we were in his upstairs bedroom.

My sister was open, too, but I sent her to Jerry Kirk who at that time was a Young Life leader in Mt. Lebanon. She, also, gave her life to Christ.

Jerry Kirk was as a young man the one who brought my two best friends in High School to the Lord. Jerry, also, went on to found the Religious Alliance against Pornography in 1986 and the 40 Day Prayer Covent and pure HOPE.

My father died saying the Lord's Prayer in the ambulance that took him to the hospital where he died.

My mother died in a home in Memphis, Tennessee.

My sister died in the Lord.

My brother followed her into the Kingdom of Heaven 3 months later.

One of my dearest friends, Barbie, who came to the Lord through Young Life in Mt. Lebanon is now with her Savior.

The other one, Diane, is still living a victorious life in Him.
Sandy, me? I'm still living by God's grace. My husband Steve and I proclaimed the Lord to our three children and raised them in "the nurture and admonition of the Lord." Kathy, Blake and Jesse all call Jesus, Savior and Lord of their lives. We are extremely blessed to have believing children. After living with Him and for Him since 1955 at the Beginning of L'Abri, I am even MORE committed to telling family, friends and street strangers in America, Central America and Europe about our Lord Jesus and the REALITY, THE EXISTENCE OF A PERSONAL GOD—THE GREAT "I AM."

"YAHWEH/JEHOVAH" means "I AM THAT I AM."

GOD really IS.

A Visit to L'Abri After I Left

My first visit to L'Abri after I left was 15 years later in May of 1971. My first husband and I had divorced and I fled for shelter to Lausanne, Switzerland with my two young children: 8 year-old Kathy and 5 year-old Blake. I was 33 years old. My children and I went up to L'Abri from Lausanne and stayed with the Schaeffer's daughter Priscilla, her husband John Sandri and their young children. I had known Priscilla and John very well in my year at L'Abri. They were now married and lived in a L'Abri chalet near to the original L'Abri Chalet Les Melezes.

At that time the Schaeffer children had moved Fran and Edith into an apartment near Montreux on Lake Geneva. The children had furnished the apartment with some furniture Fran and Edith had when they were first married. Apparently the Schaeffers' work which had begun 16 years earlier in 1955 was beginning to fray their marriage and the Schaeffer children felt they needed to be alone.

When I knew the Schaeffers in 1955-56, they seemed to be independent people who were married. By that I mean I never saw them together. Edith was always doing something here and Schaeffer was doing something there. Except at the dinner table, they were always separate. They never sat next to each other on the couch or hugged or smiled a special smile to each other. I can understand that because their home was always filled with people when I was there. They were a "team" and I never saw them "riled or annoyed" with each other. However, I know the demands on them must have made them "fight" from time to time. But I/we, of course, would never have seen that.

Edith told me several times about how they met. They did not know each other but both attended a church meeting where the preacher was saying things she thought were not true. She stood up and defended the Biblical position. Then Fran jumped up and defended it, too. Edith sat down while Fran continued to refute and rebuke the liberal speaker. After the "service," they met, walked home together and the rest is history, as they say. Or as Edith would say: "There are no accidental meetings. There are only Providential meetings."

After I left L'ABRI at that visit, Priscilla told her parents I was there and all about my circumstances. Schaeffer wanted to set up a meeting with me in Montreux. When we met by Lake Geneva, my children played around us a small distance from where we talked.

I explained to Schaeffer how my husband Jack and I had for several years a ministry to kids who were hooked on drugs. Many had come to the Lord and many had not, but every Wednesday night about 50 young people showed up at our home. I and others from our church provided snacks for them.

Francis & Edith Schaeffer – their vows July 6, 1935

It was wonderful to see how the Lord could save/rescue teens and others from LSD, alcohol, heroine and methadone which doctors who thought they were "helping" kids were prescribing to them. The kids told me those methadone "biscuits," as they called them, were selling on the street as well as and at the same price as heroine. But the clutch of the Evil One was severed in many kids. Jack and my marriage was, also, broken up.

Schaeffer totally understood the dynamic and was comforting to me. He suggested I come back to L'Abri and work with him on some of his many projects. I and my children could live with them. I did not accept his kind invitation.

It was during that time with Schaeffer on the shores of Lake Geneva that I kept referring to my guilt over the divorce. Schaeffer asked me, "Have you confessed your sins to the Lord?" "Of course. I had constantly asked Him for forgiveness," I said.

Schaeffer said to me: "If you have confessed your sin to the Lord and taken His forgiveness, if a confessed and forgiven sin in my life comes up again, here's what I do. I image the devil as a big black dog who has his paws on my shoulders. I say to him, 'Get your dirty paws off of me!'"

He explained to me that confessed and forgiven-by-God sins are to God as far away as the east is from the west. It's the devil who doesn't want us to forget, to be bound by our guilt. God wants us to live a free life in Him. The devil always deals "guilt cards." Don't pick them up.

"If we confess our sins, He is faithful and just to forgive us our sins and to cleanse us from all unrighteousness." 1 John 1:9

Again Schaeffer, who was going through a crisis in his own life, had just the right words at the right time in my life just as he had so many years ago when I was at L'Abri — At The Beginning. Under his tutelage and by God's grace, I had become free from the angst of existentialism and became a grateful slave to Christ. (Philippians 1:1 "Paul and Timothy, servants of Christ Jesus…" The real word for "servant" in the Greek is *doulos*, meaning "slave." The Greek word for "slave" is used over 100 times in the New Testament to refer to believers and to Paul himself. We are to see ourselves as "Bought-and-Paid-For slaves of Christ."

The Summer of c. 1982 I took a friend of my daughter, Andrea Pritchett. up to L'Abri's home in America—Southborough, Massachusetts. Our Hosts were Dick and Mardi Keyes whose L'Abri in America was filled with welcome and learning.

March 28, 2008, 53 years after I was at L'Abri, there was an article in *Christianity Today* called *"Not Your Father's L'Abri"* which disturbed me. A part of it said:

"Amelia embodies what L'Abri has become: a community ambivalent about Schaeffer's legacy and ill at ease with mainstream evangelical culture. Half a century after L'Abri's founding and more than 20 years after Schaeffer's death, students come with very different questions, and they look askance at the politicized faith that Schaeffer helped create."

Another article published by Dan Claire in 1/16/2009, 54 years after I left L'Abri, was a letter Schaeffer had supposedly written to Dan. Obviously, Schaeffer, in 2009 long dead, was describing in this letter to Dan Claire the "cost over the decades of just being L'Abri."

Francis Schaeffer on Hospitality

"Don't start with a big program. Don't suddenly think you can add to your church budget and begin. Start personally and start in your home. I dare you. I dare you in the name of Jesus Christ. Do what I am going to suggest. Begin by opening your home for community.

How many times in the past year have you risked having a drunk vomit on your carpeted floor? How in the world, then, can you talk about compassion and about community – about the church's job in the inner city?

L'Abri is costly. If you think what God has done here is easy, you don't understand. It's a costly business to have a sense of community. L'Abri cannot be explained merely by the clear doctrine that is preached; it cannot be explained by the fact that God has here been giving intellectual answers to intellectual questions. I think those two things are important, but L'Abri cannot be explained if you remove the third. And that is there has been some community here. And it has been costly.

In about the first three years of L'Abri all our wedding presents were wiped out. Our sheets were torn. Holes were burned in our rugs. Indeed once a whole curtain almost burned up from somebody smoking in our living room. Blacks came to our table. Orientals came to our table. Everybody came to our table. It couldn't happen any other way. Drugs came to our place. People vomited in our rooms, in the rooms of Chalet Les Melezes which was our home, and now in the rest of the chalets of L'Abri.

How many times has this happened to you? You see, you don't need a big program. You don't have to convince your session or board. All you have to do is open your home and begin. And there is no place in God's world where there are no people who will come and share a home as long as it is a real home."

My Husband Steve and I Go to L'Abri

I revisited L'Abri again in 2011 when my husband Steve and I went to Europe for our 40th Anniversary. I contacted Priscilla (who was then called Prisca) and her husband John (who later was called Gion). We took the bus up, up the winding road and John met us at the stop in Huemoz. We arrived around noon for the day. The three of us (Priscilla, John and I) were somewhat "taken aback" by "the ravages of time." Of course it had been 40 years since we had seen each other in 1971 and 56 years since the start of L'Abri when we were teens together.

Priscilla prepared Raclette for us. To me, it was Fondue but over the decades it had become Raclette. In my days in Switzerland in the 1950's Raclettes were the crispy leavings on the fondue bowl which one scrapped off at the end of the Fondue meal. Her meal was delicious and served with small potatoes we dipped into the Raclette.

I wanted to show Steve Chalet Les Melezes where it all began at the Beginning of L'Abri. We walked over, entered the chalet and found it relatively EMPTY. I showed him the fireplace downstairs where Schaeffer and I had our first talk. It was an EMPTY room that day. I tried to have Steve imagine the room warm with a crackling fire and filled with eager young people asking probing questions and getting Biblical answers from Schaeffer. The room now felt really EMPTY.

Upstairs we found about 8 people of all ages. They looked on us as strangers who had wandered into their space. I told them I was there at the beginning of L'Abri. Rather than being at all curious, they were blase, were so what? I asked them what they were doing at L'Abri and they had very fuzzy answers. They then withdrew from Steve and me. They seemed to me to be a "rag-taggle bunch of teens and adults" who were not at all hospitable or even polite. I was angry. Angry those current occupants of the chalet seemed to be there for no "L'Abri reason" for being there. I asked two of them why they were there and they seemed to be there because it was "a place to stay." I was angry at what I saw had happened to my L'Abri. When they slowly left in a bunch, they faded away like ghosts.

As Steve and I wandered through the rooms of Chalet Les Melezes, I told him about what had happened in certain rooms. I remembered beautiful dark-eyed, black-haired Edith there in the kitchen preparing a Chinese meal for her family and me the first weekend I went up to L'Abri. Edith seemed to be always in the kitchen preparing meals for the many who would come to L'Abri and serving them with posies on the table or a surprise dessert. She would be talking about the Lord to whomever was helping her peel potatoes or beating up whipped cream.

I remembered the folding chairs downstairs by the fire for Sunday Services. We all lined up in rows. Either Priscilla or Edith played the piano as we sang hymns. I never had sung hymns before and was thrilled to be taught by the Biblical words in them. I like "praise music," but the old hymns I learned during Sunday Church at L'Abri I still revert to when I am alone. Schaeffer always gave a c. 30-minute sermon on some Biblical doctrine. He had such "sad eyes" I always thought, but when he preached and when he was happy, his sad eyes were happy. And if he smiled, his whole face lit up. When Church broke up, Edith gave us one of her signature "high teas."

When Steve and I went outside into the front yard, I remembered Pris, John, Murray and me playing statue there. One of the four of us whirled around the other three and we landed in crazy, awkward poses and laughed. I still have a picture of us, statue-posed, from our time together in 1955.

At the Beginning of L'Abri, it was a very fun, mentally stimulating, exciting and easy place to be. When Steve and I were there in 2011, it was filled with stone-cold statues. I was "désolé", as the French say. I was desolated, sorry at what L'Abri had become.

Schaeffer had been dead over 30 years. Priscilla said her mother Edith was still vibrant and evangelizing. When we were there in 2011, Edith was living in Gryon with her believing daughter Debby, her husband Udo Middleman and their children. Edith was just 11 minutes, a short 4.3 miles from their Chalet Les Melezes home. But it seemed to me Edith rarely came to Huemoz to see Priscilla, John and their children nor did she come to see what was going on at L'Abri.

When Priscilla and I were alone, she said there had been some sort of falling-out between her husband John and her father Francis. I almost cried as sad, strained Priscilla described the break. She was a woman who had been torn apart for years between two loves—the Family of her father Francis, her mother Edith and her siblings and the Family she and her husband and children had built together.

Priscilla's believing sister Susan and her husband had spearheaded the development of L'Abri in England. Her 3-year-old brother Franky whom I "played with" the year I was there was now called Frank and had "jumped the rails" and become a "believing atheist' (an oxymoron). The Christian community was shocked when he trashed his parents and his heritage in his book *Crazy for God*. I was not really shocked because I remembered that he was a "toddler" when I was there and Franky was doted upon. But I, also, knew he came of age in the 60's when the "sex/nickel-bag/rock 'n' roll" generation came to L'Abri in droves. L'Abri was not prepared for that, but those hipsters were a definite influence upon dear Franky.

As Edith and I were talking one day in 1956, she said to me, "We never intend our ministry here at L'Abri to continue after we are gone."

Amen. So Be It.

Edith Memorial

Even at age 18, I thought Francis Schaeffer was the Brain of L'Abri and Edith Sevillle Schaeffer was the Heart/Soul of L'Abri.

FROM—Memorial Service (FOR)
Edith Rachel Merritt Seville Schaeffer 1914—2013
Delivered by Susan Schaeffer's husband, Edith's son-in-law Ranald Macaulay MA Cantab, The Round Church, Cambridge

'Every generation produces individuals who seem larger than life. Like meteors they blaze into life and become something of a wonder to those looking on. 'What remarkable talents, 'we say, 'what energy, what achievements! 'This is what Edith Schaeffer was like and for 17 years Rochester (Minnesota) was her home.

Like many coming to the Mayo Clinic, the reasons for her arrival were hardly auspicious. Her husband, Francis, had just completed filming in Switzerland for his second major documentary series called, *Whatever Happened to the Human Race*. At the end of a grueling day on the slopes near their alpine home, his dramatic weight loss over the previous week led Edith to telephone a medical friend at Mayo to seek advice. 'Get him here as quickly as possible ' he said. So on October 9th, 1978, Edith and Francis arrived in Rochester. Within hours he had been diagnosed with lymphoma and put on chemotherapy. It was to be the beginning, for Edith certainly, of a long association with the city and its people. Happily, Francis responded well to treatment and continued to be active and influential throughout the world for another seven years. By then Edith had moved their home from Switzerland to Rochester and it was there, on May 15th, 1984, that she heard his last quiet words… "from strength to strength" – taken from the sentence 'they go from strength to strength till each appears before God in Zion 'in Psalm 84:7.

Her days as the wife of one of the world's most significant evangelical leaders in the 20th century had come to a close.
However, her surprise at finding herself living in Rochester was hardly her last! She seemed to specialize in surprises in fact. The next one came within weeks of her husband's death and through what had been the major part of her life's work, namely L'Abri Fellowship. She and her husband had founded this Christian work in Switzerland in 1955 and one of its half-dozen branches (now ten world-wide) had moved from California to Rochester to provide,

amongst other things, practical support for them in their medical need. Not long after the funeral in Rochester came the new surprise - a Steinway grand-piano no less. This was a gift to L'Abri in memory of Francis Schaeffer and it held pride of place in her gracious living room.

But the surprise contained yet another surprise and one which opened up a new chapter in her life. For what she quickly realized was that the actual piano involved, discovered not far from Rochester incidentally, had been manufactured the same year as her marriage – and came into her home July 6th, 1984, 49 years exactly after the very day she and Francis had their wedding— July 6th, 1936!

This piqued her already vibrant curiosity. So the next time she was in New York she arranged to call at the Steinway factory. Quite unexpectedly she found herself in the midst of a red-carpet-welcome and all because the company's senior piano-voicer, Franz Mohr, had for many years been one of her avid readers and admirers.

The visit began a lasting friendship and even resulted in a new book called *Forever Music*. Amongst other things it was a paean to the wonder of God's creation. It also provided her with a medium to express one of the leading characteristics of her life, namely her delight in anything and everything beautiful. She herself was a beautiful woman and always dressed impeccably. When she provided meals it became an occasion not just for good food but for a 'work of art '—hence the title of another of her books, *Hidden Art*. But *Forever Music* also described how God works into our individual lives – in this case via the biography and conversion of Franz Mohr himself. This in turn led to a concert with the Guarneri Quartet in Alice Tully Hall at the Lincoln Centre, New York, and to personal friendships with some of the world's most illustrious musicians like Rudolf Serkin, Vladimir Horowitz and Yo Yo Ma.

Her ongoing life continued to be part of the 'Rochester L'Abri 'for more than a decade and it enabled her to put her gifts of teaching, hospitality and creativity to good use. Many, for example, were the musical soirees in her living room around the Steinway. She spoke regularly at the annual Rochester L'Abri Conferences in February. But she also served as an international Trustee of L'Abri until 2001 making a grand total of 46 years within the life of the Fellowship.

She also went on with her writing. Already she had completed nearly a dozen books, some of which, like *The L'Abri Story*, *The Tapestry*, and *Christianity is Jewish* had sold almost as successfully as her husband's—as they still do. The scope of her activities went well beyond Rochester, though, both within the United States and abroad. For example, she had been instrumental in the formation of the Francis Schaeffer Foundation based in New York and Switzerland and also in the Francis Schaeffer Institute in St. Louis, an adjunct of Covenant Theological Seminary. Her speaking itinerary was extensive.

Then followed another major surprise when she returned, now aged 80, to the very place in China where she had been born. Once again she found herself the subject of an official red-carpet welcome laid on, believe it or not, by the secular city dignitaries! The third and last of three daughters born to missionary parents, she was only five when they returned to the United States. Like all her memories, however, her recollections of China remained vivid and these she put into a children's book bearing her Chinese name 'Mei Fuh'. For all her fizz and sparkle, however, and despite frequent displays of energy and creativity, even in old age, which left her younger colleagues in L'Abri breathless, the time came for her to return to her beloved Lac Leman (Lake Geneva) in Switzerland. There she lived in a flat in a small lakeside village beside Vevey where she and her husband had spent many happy years.

In due course she needed more care and one of her daughters, Mrs. Debby Middelmann (the Schaeffer's daughter Debby), with her husband, Udo, graciously provided a home in the mountains not far from where she and Francis had first founded L'Abri Fellowship in 1955. There, after a long decline in health, she died on the 30th March 2013 - aged 98.
It was a long and remarkable life – truly meteoric. But when all is said and done the best thing about Edith was who she was as a person: she never became big-headed because of her successes; she was always generous (even to a fault!); she consistently, and however inconveniently, treated all who came within her ambit with a gentleness and love both radiant and deeply genuine. In short, she was 'real'- a true Christian lady whose first desire was to glorify her Maker and Saviour.

What she and her husband took as their life-long goal was to try to demonstrate and declare to all they met that the Bible really is true and that the Judeo-Christian God is a kind and gracious Saviour to those who come to Him. She never swerved from that object. Nor, right until the day she died, did she ever flinch from the costliness of that call. She obeyed the apostolic summons to 'present your body as a living sacrifice to Christ' (Romans 12:1). And now she is with Him. Hallelujah!"

And this writer says Hallelujah, Praise God for Edith Schaeffer's long life and Praise God for the work she and Francis Schaeffer did in the Name of Christ for me, for the Body of Christ and for their Lord and Savior.

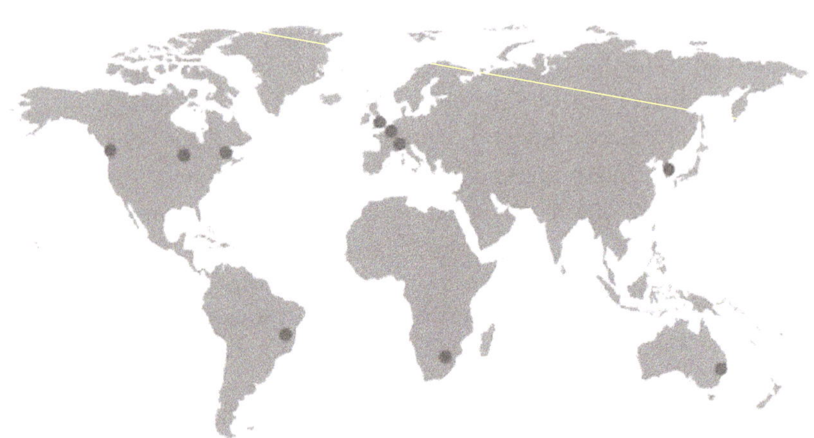

Map of L'Abri communities around the world

CHAPTER 7
SEEDS OF FAITH

Every one who comes to Christ has a story to tell. Every one who is born-again has seeds which someone or some incident had planted in her or him. Christ Himself taught in parables about "planting and planted seeds." These seeds were planted in me long before I gave my life to my Savior:

SEED 1. At age 4-5, my grandmother Meme taught me a little prayer I said every night:

"Blessed Jesus, meek and mild,
Smile upon a little child.
Pity my simplicity.
Teach me, Lord, to come to Thee."

Then, as my Mother was still sitting on the edge of my bed, I would Bless by name all the members of my family and all my relatives. During World War II, I would end the prayer with "And bless our boys who are fighting." Once my Mother said to me when I finished, "You know, Sandra, you should bless all the German and Japanese boys, too. Because they have Mothers and Fathers and children just like we do." I was shocked she said that, but then I realized that was true, so I ended my prayers from then on with: "And bless the German and Japan boys, too."
I think that was the first time I ever thought about blessing our enemies.

SEED 2. When I was 5 years old, a neighboring woman on our street in Warren, Ohio, came to our door and asked my Mother if my sister who was 3 and I could attend a Bible School she was going to have in our neighborhood that summer. My Mother was pregnant with my brother Johnny and thought that would be a nice thing for my sister and me to do week-day mornings.
Plus, my Mother was a very kind woman and that woman had no children. I remember to this day the little song the woman taught about 6 of us in her living room:

"One door and only one
And yet their sides are two.

I'm on the inside.
Which side are you?"

When our Dad got home, Tooie and I sang that song to our parents and they thought it was lovely. We all sat on the floor of that wonderful woman's living room. I can still see the carpet with its large cabbage roses in it. She gave us milk and graham crackers as she talked to us. I don't remember a thing she said. But I knew we were there to "study the Bible."
One day during that summer, she taught us another song. When we got home, we sang it to our parents. Don't remember many of the words, but it was a song about trains. I remember we had to make our little arms go back and forth as we "choo-chooed" along:

"I'm on the choo-choo train to heaven.
Are you on the choo-choo train to hell?"

That was the last time we were ever allowed to go to her home.
But she planted a strong seed in me with the *Door Song* and I have a particular fondness for Sallman's painting *Christ At The Door*—"Behold, I stand at the door, and knock: if any man hear my voice, and open the door, I will come in to him, and will sup with him, and he with me." Revelation 3:20
The door was closed with the Train Song, but 13 years later, I opened the door of my heart, mind and spirit to Jesus at L'Abri in the Swiss Alps. In Sallman's painting there is no doorknob on the outside of the door. You have to open the door from the inside. Jesus, filled with light outside the door, just keeps knocking at that door, our heart. The painting has a little window showing how dark it is inside.

SEED 3. Warren, Ohio was the county seat in our Ohio district and in the middle of our downtown there was a huge beautiful, domed big building surrounded by a large park. My Dad and I, about 8 years old, were walking the sidewalks of that park. He was talking and I was looking down at the sidewalk. Suddenly, he grabbed my chin and threw my head up. "Goddamnit, Sandy, look up! Always look up! If you look down, all you're going to find is money and paper and dirty things. If you look up, you'll find God and love and beauty." We kept walking and my neck hurt, but I knew my Dad was telling me something important. Beauty and God were up and things that were down were not good. When my Dad died, he was yelling out the Lord's Prayer as he looked up to the ceiling of the ambulance.

SEED 4. Every summer I went to Zaleski, Ohio and stayed with my grandmother Meme, my father's mother. Zaleski is a town in southern Ohio with a population of c. 300 people when I spent my 4-12 year-old summers there. I just looked up the population of Zaleski and as of the last census in 2010 it has only 280 people. I loved going from my medium-sized city in northern Ohio to this tiny village where everyone spoke with a Southern accent. They said "Y'all" and the "aint" word which I was taught was improper and "low-class." In fact, that whole small village was evenly composed of "us" and "them." "Us" were Meme, her friends there and people in our family. "Them" were the "low class" people. I had no idea what "low class" was. All the people I saw there seemed to me to be just regular people like we all were. One summer I saw a girl on the brick sidewalk and we looked at each other and smiled. I asked Meme to invite her to our home so I could play with her. Her name I learned was Cappy Kay. Meme told me I wasn't allowed to play with Cappy Kay because she and her family were "low class." I was sad because I had nobody my age to play with and I didn't care if she was "low class."

But that is not one of my "seeds to faith" even though it is probably the origin of my "egalitarianism."

One summer day I was sitting on Meme's front porch and heard wonderful singing coming from the store across the street that used to be boarded up. I was barefoot and crossed the newly-tarred street and stood at the entrance to the singing. I watched as a bunch of about 25 people were singing and raising their hands. There was a man in front of them who had a book in his hands and was leading the people. He saw me and said, "Little girl, would you like to come in?" I said, "yes" and went in all the way up to the first row where no one was sitting. They were singing about Jesus and some would say, "Hallelujah" or clap their hands. I loved being there with all these happy people. The man in front said, "Let's now open our Bibles" to a place I had never heard of. He took his Bible in his hands and started talking about this Jesus. I noticed his Bible was like taffy in his hands because it bent all the way down on both sides as he held it. I don't remember a word of what the Bible man said, but I do remember this:

My Meme shouted at me from the door of the building in a loud and mad voice, "Sandra, get out of this place and come to me immediately!" I looked at the Bible man and he said, "You'd better go now." I got up and walked down the aisle and all the people in folding chairs on either side of me looked at me. When I stepped outside, Meme took me by my arm and kept saying, "Why in God's name would you ever go into that church? Those people are low class and you don't belong there." We went into her home. I don't remember what punishment she gave me. Maybe I wasn't allowed that day to take some pennies from the sewing basket and go next door to Batchie's and get candy. I don't remember. But I do remember those people singing about Jesus and being so happy and that Bible man with his Bible like taffy.

SEED 5. I have written about my confirmation at age 12 in a church where the minister put the sign of the cross on my forehead and it burned me and I can still feel the slight warming if I think or write of that time.

SEED 6. As I have mentioned, when we were in high school two of my best friends, Barbie and Diane called "Dutch." gave their lives to Christ through a group called Young Life. They were excited but I was not impressed. They couldn't answer any of my questions and when they took me to their leader, he could not answer questions to my satisfaction either. Barbie died recently of breast cancer. All during her treatments she was cheerful and reaching out to others getting chemotherapy beside her and telling them of Christ. My other friend, Dutch, who gave her life to Christ in high school still loves Him and evangelizes others.

SEED 7. The boy in my senior year who gave me his Bible and challenged me to read the four Gospels. I did and did not believe in Christ. But the Gospel Word had been planted in me.

SEED 8. As I have recounted, our dog Teddy Cochoran died and I was comforted by the new white Bible my boyfriend (bought by his mother) had given me for High School Graduation. Just flipped it open and put my finger on a verse. It was Revelation 5:13:

"And every creature which is in heaven, and on the earth, and under the earth, and such as are in the sea, and all that are in them, heard I saying, Blessing, and honour, and glory, and power, be unto him that sitteth upon the throne, and unto the Lamb for ever and ever."
I KNEW Teddy was in heaven and that comforted me and I stopped crying.

All the seeds in me of the Bible and of Christ came to fruition at L'Abri in the Fall of 1955 where I gave my life and eternity to Christ.

What is your story? Where were you and who were the SOWERS who planted in you and when did those tiny seeds grow, become visible above the earth and produce a crop?

Jesus explained to His disciples:

"But the seed falling on good soil refers to someone who hears the word and understands it. This is the one who produces a crop, yielding a hundred, sixty or thirty times what was sown." Matthew 13:23

APPENDIX
SCHAEFFER STUDY RESOURCES

To further explore the teachings and ministry of Francis Schaeffer, contact Bruce Little at Southeastern Baptist Theological Seminary.

BRUCE A. LITTLE
Emeritus Professor of Philosophy
Director of the Francis A. Schaeffer Collection

Southeastern Baptist Theological Seminary
OUR MISSION: Southeastern Baptist Theological Seminary seeks to glorify the Lord Jesus Christ by equipping students to serve the Church and fulfill the Great Commission.

120 S. Wingate St • Wake Forest, NC 27587 • Phone: (919) 761-2100

EDUCATION
B.R.E., Baptist Bible College
M.A., M.A.R., Liberty University
D. Min., Columbia Biblical Seminary
Ph.D., Southeastern Baptist Theological Seminary

The Francis A Schaeffer Collection—Bruce Little, Director

Francis A. Schaeffer Papers: An Overview, 2015

The Library at Southeastern
114 N. Wingate Street
Wake Forest, NC 27587

"Digital copies of the papers and audio recordings are also available for approved researchers at the Francis A. Schaeffer Foundation headquarters in Gyron, Switzerland and the Hill House in Austin, Texas.

Inquiries about research at the Francis A. Schaeffer Foundation should be directed to Udo Middelmann. Inquiries about research at the Hill House (in Austin, Texas) should be directed to Greg Grooms. See our policies and procedures governing research inquiries for more information about requesting permission to access the Francis A. Schaeffer Papers at Southeastern Baptist Theological Seminary.

Francis A. Schaeffer Studies at Southeastern: Francis A. Schaeffer Collection Information on the unique resources and opportunities at Southeastern Baptist Theological Seminary supporting the study of Francis A. Schaeffer's life, work, and thought.

Home
Francis A. Schaeffer Collection | Toggle Dropdown
Francis A. Schaeffer Society
Library at Southeastern Resources | Toggle Dropdown
Additional Resources | Toggle Dropdown
Contact Us

Francis A. Schaeffer Collection at Southeastern
Southeastern Baptist Theological Seminary (SEBTS) serves as the research home for the preeminent collection of personal papers documenting the life and ministry of Francis A. Schaeffer. This collection of correspondence, manuscripts, notes, annotated books and periodicals, audio recordings, and other materials created by Schaeffer during his ministry was given in custodianship to SEBTS by the Francis A. Schaeffer Foundation, which maintains ownership. Since receiving the collection, SEBTS Archives & Digitization Lab staff have processed the collection and created digital copies of all the papers and audio recordings it contains. **SEBTS students and faculty, as well as, members of the broader research community with an interest in Christian apologetics, evangelism, cultural studies, worldview thinking, and the life and work of Francis A. Schaeffer are encouraged to take advantage of this unique resource and plan a research visit.**

The collection is open for research at three approved research sites. The original materials and digital copies are available for approved researchers at SEBTS. **Digital copies of the papers and audio recordings are also available for approved researchers at the Francis A. Schaeffer Foundation headquarters in Gyron, Switzerland and the Hill House in Austin, Texas.**

A finding aid for the collection, including an item-level inventory, is available to help plan your research. Work is currently underway to optimize the descriptions in the inventory for digital research and create a searchable database for these resources. Updates to the inventory will be added on a regular basis.

Please note that the Francis A. Schaeffer Foundation has restricted access to the three research sites listed above and requires that researchers apply for permission to access the Francis A. Schaeffer Papers. Inquiries about research at the Francis A. Schaeffer Foundation should be directed to Udo Middelmann. Inquiries about research at the Hill House should be directed to Greg Grooms. See our policies and procedures governing research inquiries for more information about requesting permission to access the Francis A. Schaeffer Papers at Southeastern Baptist Theological Seminary."

www.ingramcontent.com/pod-product-compliance
Lightning Source LLC
Chambersburg PA
CBHW061339120726
48001CB00002B/949